BRINGING BACK THE

Grizzly Bear

Ruth Daly

CRABTREE
PUBLISHING COMPANY
WWW.CRABTREEBOOKS.COM

CRABTREE
PUBLISHING COMPANY
WWW.CRABTREEBOOKS.COM

Author: Ruth Daly

Series Research and Development: Reagan Miller

Managing Editor: Tim Cooke

Picture Manager: Sophie Mortimer

Design Manager: Keith Davis

Editorial Director: Lindsey Lowe

Children's Publisher: Anne O'Daly

Editor: Ellen Rodger

Proofreader: Lorna Notsch

Cover design: Margaret Amy Salter

Production coordinator and
   Prepress technician: Margaret Amy Salter

Print coordinator: Katherine Berti

Produced for Crabtree Publishing Company
by Brown Bear Books

Photographs (t=top, b= bottom, l=left, r=right, c=center)

Front Cover: All images from Shutterstock

Interior: Alamy: BLM Photo, 18, Christopher B, 13t, Minden Pictures, 5, NPS Photo, 28, David Tipling 10; Craighead Institute: Craighead Family, 15tl; Dreamstime: Vladimir Chech, 26; Getty Images: David Nevala, 14; iStock: Clayton Andersen, 21, blazer76, 15r, Hung Chung Chih, 27b, PX Hildago, 27tr, roundhill, 29, skyhobo, 24, WestwindPhoto, 1, 7; Shutterstock: Bobs Creek Photography, 17, Samuel Cornstein, 8, Chase Dekker, 25b, Ronnie Howard, 20–21, Mikluhua Maklai, 9br, tome Reichner, 25t, Sergey Uryadnikov, 4; Staticflickr.com: 13b; USA.gov: IGSBST/USGS/National Parks Photo, 16–17, Richard Sniezko/U.S. Forest Service, 9t, Suzanna Soileau/USGS, 19b, USFWS, 6-7, USFWS Mountain Prairie, 12; Wyoming Fish and Game Reserve: Mark Gocke, 22; Yale Education: Louisa Willcox, 19r.

Brown Bear Books has made every attempt to contact the copyright holder. If you have any information please contact licensing@brownbearbooks.co.uk

Library and Archives Canada Cataloguing in Publication

Daly, Ruth, 1962-, author
      Bringing back the grizzly bear / Ruth Daly.

(Animals back from the brink)
Includes index.
Issued in print and electronic formats.
ISBN 978-0-7787-4904-2 (hardcover).--
ISBN 978-0-7787-4910-3 (softcover).--
ISBN 978-1-4271-2104-2 (HTML)

      1. Grizzly bear--Juvenile literature. 2. Grizzly bear--Conservation--Juvenile literature. 3. Endangered species--Juvenile literature. 4. Wildlife recovery--Juvenile literature. I. Title.

QL737.C27D25 2018   j333.95'978416   C2018-903051-8
                                                    C2018-903052-6

Library of Congress Cataloging-in-Publication Data

Names: Daly, Ruth, 1962- author.
Title: Bringing back the grizzly bear / Ruth Daly.
Description: New York, New York : Crabtree Publishing, [2019] | Series: Animals back from the brink | Includes index.
Identifiers: LCCN 2018036858 (print) | LCCN 2018037481 (ebook) | ISBN 9781427121042 (Electronic) | ISBN 9780778749042 (hardcover : alk. paper) | ISBN 9780778749103 (paperback : alk. paper)
Subjects: LCSH: Grizzly bear--United States--Conservation--Juvenile literature.
Classification: LCC QL737.C27 (ebook) | LCC QL737.C27 D289 2019 (print) | DDC 599.784--dc23
LC record available at https://lccn.loc.gov/2018036858

Crabtree Publishing Company
www.crabtreebooks.com   1-800-387-7650

Printed in the U.S.A./102018/CG20180810

Published in Canada
Crabtree Publishing
616 Welland Ave.
St. Catharines, Ontario
L2M 5V6

Published in the United States
Crabtree Publishing
PMB 59051
350 Fifth Avenue, 59th Floor
New York, New York 10118

Published in the United Kingdom
Crabtree Publishing
Maritime House
Basin Road North, Hove
BN41 1WR

Published in Australia
Crabtree Publishing
3 Charles Street
Coburg North
VIC, 3058

Contents

Find videos and extra material online at **crabtreeplus.com** to learn more about the conservation of animals and ecosystems. See page 30 in this book for the access code to this material.

Grizzly Bears in Danger

Grizzly bears are one of the great symbols of the **wilderness**. They have an enormous **range** in North America, from the Arctic in the north to the far western provinces in Canada and the northwestern United States. A large population of grizzlies lives in Yellowstone National Park in Wyoming. Most visitors to Yellowstone hope to catch sight of these **reclusive** animals. About 700 grizzly bears now live within the park, but it has not always been this way. During the 1900s, their numbers steadily **declined**. By 1975, only 136 grizzlies remained in the Yellowstone region.

Grizzly bears are powerful hunters with excellent senses of sight, sound, and smell. They can run at speeds of up to 35 to 40 miles per hour (55–65 km/h) and can climb trees. Grizzly bears are larger than black bears, and can be distinguished by the muscle on their back that gives them a humplike appearance.

FOOD, GLORIOUS FOOD

During the 1900s, people built settlements in the bears' natural habitat. Bear attacks on people, livestock, and pets rose. Hunting and trapping were legal ways for people to deal with troublesome bears. Grizzly bears are **omnivores**. Their varied diet includes whitebark-pine nuts, cutthroat trout, army cutworm moths, and **species** of roots and berries. Yellowstone grizzlies traditionally ate more meat than grizzly bears elsewhere because the park is home to so much **prey**. However, despite the natural food sources, over the last century, the grizzly bear population gradually became dependent on **artificial** food sources left by people, which were easier to find than having to hunt. Bears have excellent memories. They remember where they found food in the past and return to the same place. Instead of hunting and **foraging**, they ate at garbage dumps, raided dumpsters and campsites, and killed **livestock** on nearby farms.

It was a common sight to see cars parked along the roads through the park in Yellowstone as people fed the bears and took pictures.

Species at Risk

Created in 1984, the International Union for the **Conservation** of Nature (IUCN) protects wildlife, plants, and **natural resources** around the world. Its members include about 1,400 governments and nongovernmental organizations. The IUCN publishes the Red List of Threatened Species each year, which tells people how likely a plant or animal species is to become **extinct**. It began publishing the list in 1964.

The golden toad of Costa Rica was last recorded by the IUCN in 1989, and is now classed as Extinct (EX). The IUCN updates the Red List twice a year to track the changing of species. Each individual species is reevaluated at least every five years.

SCIENTIFIC CRITERIA

The Red List, created by scientists, divides nearly 80,000 species of plants and animals into nine categories. Criteria for each category include the growth and **decline** of the population size of a species. They also include how many individuals within a species can breed, or have babies. In addition, scientists include information about the habitat of the species, such as its size and quality. These criteria allow scientists to figure out the probability of extinction facing the species.

IUCN LEVELS OF THREAT

The Red List uses nine categories to define the threat to a species.

Extinct (EX)	No living individuals survive
Extinct in the Wild (EW)	Species cannot be found in its natural habitat. Exists only in **captivity**, in **cultivation**, or in an area that is not its natural habitat.
Critically Endangered (CR)	At extremely high risk of becoming extinct in the wild
Endangered (EN)	At very high risk of extinction in the wild
Vulnerable (VU)	At high risk of extinction in the wild
Near Threatened (NT)	Likely to become threatened in the near future
Least Concern (LC)	Widespread, abundant, or at low risk
Data Deficient (DD)	Not enough data to make a judgment about the species
Not Evaluated (NE)	Not yet evaluated against the criteria

In the United States, the Endangered Species Act of 1973 was passed to protect species from possible extinction. It has its own criteria for classifying species, but they are similar to those of the IUCN. Canada introduced the Species at Risk Act in 2002. More than 530 species are protected under the act. The list of species is compiled by the Committee on the Status of Endangered Wildlife in Canada (COSEWIC).

GRIZZLY BEARS AT RISK

The IUCN Red List classifies grizzly bears as Least Concern. This is based on the global population. In the United States, grizzlies were listed as Near Threatened in 1975. However, by 2018 the population in Yellowstone had grown, and the bear was **delisted** there. In 2012, it was listed as of Special Concern in Canada.

Where Have All the Bears Gone?

Before the expansion of U.S. settlement in the 1800s, grizzly bears roamed throughout North America. The bears lived in forests, meadows, and wetlands, but in the 1880s, the land was changed by settlers who built farms, towns, railroads, and roads. By 1930, the range of the grizzlies was 2 percent of what it had been. Within 200 years, the grizzly bear population in the lower 48 states fell from about 50,000 to between 800 and 1,000. Habitat loss and hunting led to the bears being listed as Threatened on the IUCN Red List.

As the habitat of grizzly bears was reduced by human settlement, food sources such as elk and bison also fell. Bears strayed onto farms searching for food, killing livestock. People solved the problem by hunting, poisoning, and trapping bears, which for much of the 1900s was legal.

Some reductions in the food sources available to grizzlies had natural causes. An infestation of the mountain pine beetle steadily killed thousands of whitebark pine trees, which affected the supply of pine nuts that the bears eat. The nuts contain high amounts of fat and protein, and help bears fatten up for their winter hibernation, or sleep.

GARBAGE DUMPS AND BEAR JAMS

Bears began to eat garbage in Yellowstone as early as the 1880s. The bears raided dumpsters behind hotels and ate food from open-pit dumps. After World War II (1939–1945), Yellowstone became more popular with tourists, which produced more garbage for the bears. The problem was reduced by closing open-pit dumps and introducing bear-proof dumpsters. Visitors impacted bears in other ways, too. When bears were sighted along roadways, traffic would stop. These became known as "bear jams," and people would even feed bears from their cars. More roads and more traffic meant that collisions between cars and bears increased, adding yet another hazard for the grizzlies.

Trouble in the Park

The drop in grizzly bear numbers in Yellowstone threatened to damage the whole **ecosystem** of the park. When the bears dig in the soil for food, such as insects, roots, and nuts, they help air to get into the soil. The nitrogen from air makes the soil healthier, which helps plants to grow. Bears also disperse seeds through their droppings. Plants rely on animals to spread their seeds so that they can survive in an ecosystem. Grizzly bears are an **umbrella species**. This means that if an ecosystem has everything that bears need to survive, then other species can also live there easily.

Grizzlies suffered from a variety of disruptions in the ecosystem of Yellowstone. When lake trout were illegally introduced into the Yellowstone River, for example, the newcomers fed on the young cutthroat trout that form a key part of the bears' diet. Grizzlies found themselves short of food.

GRIZZLIES AND OTHER ANIMALS

Grizzly bears have an impact on many other animals in the park. They keep the **ungulate** population under control by preying on moose and elk calves, as well as old, weak, and injured animals. If there are too many ungulates, the land gets overgrazed. This results in fewer plants, which can lead to smaller populations of birds. In addition, grizzly bears often leave food behind after they have eaten. This food is eaten by **scavenger** animals such as raccoons, which scavenge **carrion** from **carcasses** left by other **predators**.

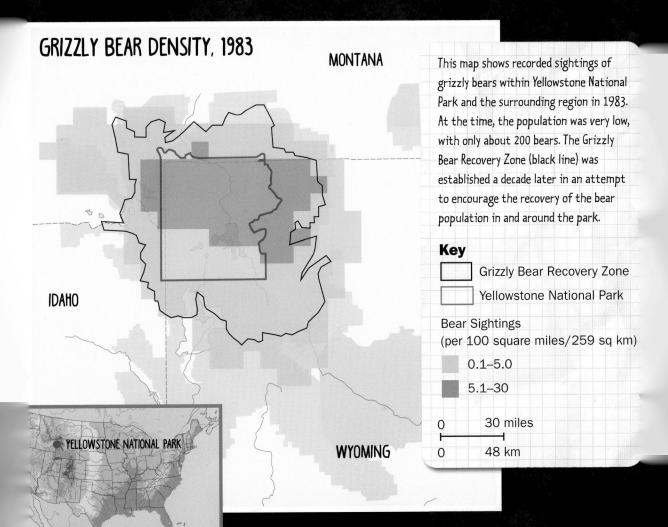

GRIZZLY BEAR DENSITY, 1983

MONTANA

IDAHO

YELLOWSTONE NATIONAL PARK

WYOMING

This map shows recorded sightings of grizzly bears within Yellowstone National Park and the surrounding region in 1983. At the time, the population was very low, with only about 200 bears. The Grizzly Bear Recovery Zone (black line) was established a decade later in an attempt to encourage the recovery of the bear population in and around the park.

Key

☐ Grizzly Bear Recovery Zone

☐ Yellowstone National Park

Bear Sightings
(per 100 square miles/259 sq km)

■ 0.1–5.0

■ 5.1–30

0   30 miles

0   48 km

Science to the Rescue!

In 1973, in response to the decline of the grizzly bear population, the U.S. government appointed a group of scientists to **monitor** the bears. This was called the Interagency Grizzly Bear Study Team. In 1975, the U.S. Fish and Wildlife Service declared grizzly bears a Threatened species in the lower 48 states. It listed grizzlies under the Endangered Species Act, which had been passed in 1973.

Being listed meant that grizzly bears would receive whatever resources were necessary to help them become **self-sustaining** again. The main requirement was a safe and secure habitat with plentiful sources of food. The U.S. Fish and Wildlife Service also put a plan into place to educate visitors about bear behavior. Many park visitors were not familiar with bears. They put themselves and the bears in danger, for example, by trying to feed the grizzlies.

A ranger of the U.S. Fish and Wildlife Service with a **tranquilized** grizzly bear. The U.S. Fish and Wildlife Service was founded to protect and conserve fish, wildlife, and plants, and the habitats in which the animals and plants live.

The Defenders of Wildlife organization took a lead role in helping grizzly bears. It was established in 1947 in Washington, D.C., and works with landowners, corporations, and state and tribal groups nationwide to protect and restore wildlife and plants to their natural habitats.

COLLABORATING FOR A CAUSE

Defenders of Wildlife was committed to providing a safe and secure environment where the grizzly bear population could grow. Involving local people and visitors was vital to the plan. The group created informative literature and posters (right). It wanted to teach anyone who came into contact with bears how to be "bear aware." The organization also introduced a system to pay ranchers **compensation** if bears attacked their livestock. The organization wanted to change the way that bears were perceived from being **nuisance** predators to being valued and worth saving.

Bringing Back the Grizzlies

The U.S. Fish and Wildlife Service made several changes to bear management in Yellowstone. It introduced a ban on hunting. People were also no longer allowed to feed bears. They had to dispose of garbage in bear-proof dumpsters and bins. To lessen encounters between people and bears, trails and hiking areas were closed in areas where bears were known to be active. This would reduce bear attacks and would also allow the bears more space in which to roam. Areas with many elk and bison were also closed to the general public because the prey attracted hungry bears.

The hunting ban made it illegal to kill grizzly bears in and around Yellowstone National Park for sport, food, or for any other reason. The law was strictly enforced, with **penalties** and fines for anyone who was caught hunting bears.

WHAT'S ON THE MENU?

Bears prepare for hibernation by eating a lot of food in the fall. When they emerge from their dens (below) the following spring, they are hungry. Both these seasons can lead to conflicts with people as the grizzlies search for food. They take fruit from orchards, honey from beehives, chickens, livestock, and even pet food. Bears also damage fences and other farm property in their quest for food.

Bear researchers John and Frank Craighead worried that removing food sources such as dumpsters might increase conflict between bears and people. They thought bears would seek food in places they associated with people, such as farmland. This did happen at first, but after a couple of years, the bears went back to foraging in the wild.

COLLABORATING FOR A CAUSE

Defenders of Wildlife hoped to make ranchers more tolerant of bears by offering financial compensation for losses due to bear activity. They believed that teaching people to be more tolerant of bears would eventually lead to fewer bears being killed. One of their innovations was to come up with a way to share the financial cost of compensating ranchers with individual Americans who were interested in conservation.

Time to Take Action

The U.S. government created the Interagency Grizzly Bear Study Team in 1973. It is made up of different government agencies working together and sharing their research on bears. Their main purpose is to observe what the bears ate and how they behaved. Careful monitoring shows where bears are located throughout an area. In 1983, the Interagency Grizzly Bear Committee was established to act on the findings.

The committee includes representatives from the states of Wyoming, Montana, and Idaho, as well as representatives from national parks and forests, scientists, biologists, and tribal leaders. One of its roles is to maintain the bears' habitat and improve it as necessary. The committee works to minimize conflicts between bears and people, and to find solutions when conflicts occurred. This group is also responsible for educating the public and conducting bear research on an ongoing basis.

CHALLENGES TO RECOVERY

In the 1980s and 1990s, studies all found that the main factor consistently bringing bears and people into conflict was food. Over many years, the Yellowstone grizzlies had adapted their diet, so that when one source ran out, they simply found something else. Between 1975 and 2000, there was an excellent supply of cutthroat trout, elk, bison, moths, and many whitebark-pine nuts. However, since 2000, these resources have steadily declined. Huge areas of whitebark pine trees have been destroyed by the mountain pine beetle and blister-rust fungus. In addition, fewer elk and bison are found roaming in the park.

Planning a recovery program relied on gathering accurate information about the grizzly population. Researchers tranquilized bears to fit them with collars that gave off a radio signal, allowing the animals' movements to be tracked. Information about **sows** and cubs helped show whether the grizzly bear population was growing, while other figures revealed how many bears were still dying from people-related causes.

Raising Funds for Action

Money for the grizzly-bear recovery program comes from a range of sources. Defenders of Wildlife set up the Bailey Wildlife Foundation Proactive Carnivore Conservation Fund in 1999. The fund has spent about $230,000 on projects to cut down on conflicts between people and bears. These include installing electric fences on farms and purchasing bear-proof dumpsters. Financing for the projects is shared among individual donors, corporations, agencies from state and federal governments, and tribes. Another fund, the Bailey Wildlife Grizzly Bear Compensation Trust, has paid more than $120,000 to ranchers whose cattle and sheep have been killed by grizzlies.

One way to prevent grizzly bears from damaging property and attacking farm animals is to install electric fences. The fences keep the bears away from areas with livestock. They also protect orchards and beehives, which attract bears with the availability of fruit and honey.

COLLABORATING FOR A CAUSE

Many conservationists have been involved in working to restore and protect the grizzly bear population. Louisa Willcox (below) has spent more than 30 years working on conservation issues, including a period as program director with the Greater Yellowstone Coalition. When a gold mine was proposed close to the park, she helped have it rejected. In 2007, when grizzly bears were removed from the Endangered Species Act, Willcox studied the whitebark pine forest. She found that many trees had been destroyed by beetles, which would damage the bears' diet. As a result, grizzly bears were put back on the endangered list.

Biologists have linked the nutrients in whitebark-pine nuts to healthy pregnancies in grizzly bears. Some research indicates that sows consuming large quantities of the nutritious pine nuts give birth to litters of three, rather than two, cubs.

The Bears Are Back!

Cooperation between conservationists and agencies gradually worked. Bears were prevented from getting non-natural food sources, and protecting their habitat reduced conflicts with people. Gradually, there was a change in public attitude away from wanting to get rid of the bears and toward conservation. People began to learn how to share the land with them. Today, the population of grizzly bears in Yellowstone has grown to about 700. Some researchers believe it may be too big for the range in Yellowstone. This might again put pressure on the delicate ecosystem of the park.

A healthy population of grizzly bears should be able to survive difficult situations such as disease, shortages of food, or even a natural disaster such as a wildfire. Long-term survival depends partly on the size of the bear population and also how easily it can connect with other groups of grizzly bears.

SUCCESS BY THE NUMBERS

It took approximately 40 years and the cooperation of several organizations to improve the outlook for grizzly bears in the Yellowstone region. The number of sows reproducing is now stable, and the grizzly bear population has increased from 136 in 1975 to around 700 in 2016. The bears have expanded their habitat by more than 50 percent. There are other interesting statistics. Between 1973 and 2004, more than 70 percent of known grizzly bear deaths were caused by people. Some were mistakenly killed by hunters and others by people defending themselves. By 2016, the figure had fallen by about 10 percent. There is more good news! The number of incidents of property damage that resulted in financial claims was reduced from approximately 200 in the 1960s to fewer than 20 incidents in the 2000s.

The rising numbers of bears in Yellowstone has led to concerns that this could lead to conflicts between bears. Bears sometimes fight over food and territory. In addition, if bears begin to range farther in search of food, this could result in them once again having more contact with people.

Looking to the Future

Concerns remain about the grizzly bear population of Yellowstone. These bears are separate from other grizzly bear populations in North America, so they could become weaker due to **genetic** inbreeding. One solution might be to create wildlife corridors to link Yellowstone with other bear communities. Changes in climate have also affected some of the bears' sources of food. Milder winters have allowed the mountain pine beetle to spread, causing serious damage to pine trees. Also, warmer temperatures mean that grizzly bears hibernate later in the fall. This increases the risk of conflicts with hunters.

Monitoring grizzly bears and their habitat costs between $4 million and $5 million each year. The money is used for many things, including radio collars, aircraft for flying over the bears' habitat, and providing or replacing bear-proof dumpsters and bins in Yellowstone.

COLLABORATING FOR A CAUSE

The Interagency Grizzly Bear Study Team includes experts from many different areas. It gathers information on sows and their cubs, and where they are living. The team observes grizzly bears in their habitat, either by hiking through wilderness areas or by flying over the park. They attach radio collars to the bears to track where they move, how long they stay in each area, and when they die. All this information helps to build a picture of the bears. From this, the agencies that manage the park learn the range of each bear and its age. This information can help park managers know when there are too many bears in an area or predict when a problem might arise.

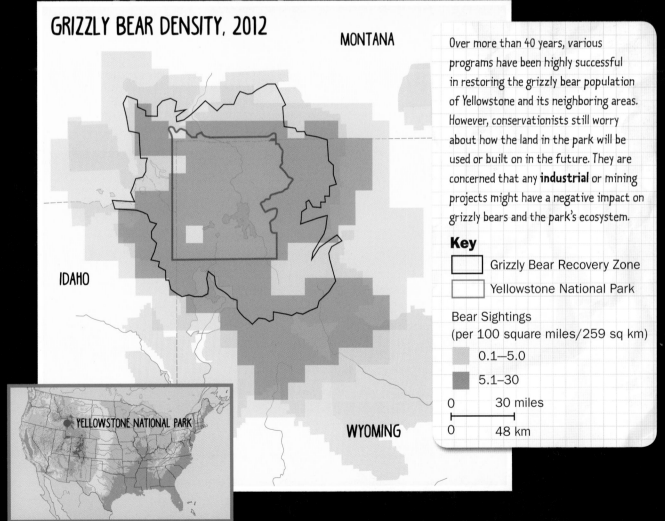

GRIZZLY BEAR DENSITY, 2012

MONTANA

IDAHO

WYOMING

Over more than 40 years, various programs have been highly successful in restoring the grizzly bear population of Yellowstone and its neighboring areas. However, conservationists still worry about how the land in the park will be used or built on in the future. They are concerned that any **industrial** or mining projects might have a negative impact on grizzly bears and the park's ecosystem.

Key

☐ Grizzly Bear Recovery Zone

☐ Yellowstone National Park

Bear Sightings
(per 100 square miles/259 sq km)

☐ 0.1—5.0

☐ 5.1–30

| 0 | 30 miles |
| 0 | 48 km |

YELLOWSTONE NATIONAL PARK

U.S. Fish and Wildlife Service removed the Yellowstone grizzly bears from protected status under the Endangered Species Act. This is known as delisting. Some people see this as a success story, because it means the bears were no longer considered to be in danger. Other people are concerned that the grizzly population will decline because the bears are no longer protected. Conservationists, scientists, and native tribal leaders have differing opinions from the Fish and Wildlife Service and other state and federal organizations.

Even though the bears of Yellowstone National Park have been removed from the endangered list, they are still carefully managed. Large areas of the park are sometimes closed to prevent contact between bears and people.

AREA BEYOND THIS SIGN
CLOSED
BEAR MANAGEMENT AREA

REASONS FOR DELISTING

- The bear population has increased so much that the habitat is no longer large enough for them all to live there safely. Male grizzlies are killing cubs because there is not enough space or food for them all.

- Delisting means grizzly bears can be hunted outside the national park. This will boost the local economy and will help control the bear population.

- Bear management has become the responsibility of the three states that make up the Yellowstone ecosystem. They have plans to closely monitor the bears. The grizzlies can always be listed again if their numbers start to fall.

REASONS AGAINST DELISTING

- Grizzly bear habitat could be reduced by construction around the park. Less space for bears leads to an increase in conflicts with people.

- Although the grizzly bear population has grown, some conservationists believe it is not stable and still needs to be protected.

- The population could decrease again if just a small number of bears are removed from the population.

- Grizzly bears have a slow **life cycle**. They do not breed until they are between at least four and 10 years old. On average, grizzlies have two cubs once every three years. If hunting is allowed again, fewer bears might reach breeding age.

Saving Other Species

Lessons learned in the fight to save the Yellowstone grizzly bears might be useful in protecting other species. The bears were found to be safer when they had minimum contact with humans. Making the bears' habitat safer was also vital. Hunting was banned, logging reduced, and trails restricted. This created a larger range for the bears. Education and compensation made tourists, ranchers, and local people more tolerant of the bears. Cooperation among government agencies, tribal groups, and conservation organizations ensured that these things happened. Although the groups did not always agree, they worked together on key issues. The end result was that the grizzly bear population increased.

The eastern gorilla of Central Africa faces some challenges similar to those of the grizzlies. Its habitat is being destroyed, and **poaching** is a serious threat. The IUCN listed it in 2016 as Critically Endangered. Banning hunting and protecting habitat could help the species recover.

SAVING THE MUNTJAC

The Bornean yellow muntjac is a small deer that lives only in the forests of the Indonesian island of Borneo. Its status on the IUCN Red List is Near Threatened. The deers' population has declined due to habitat loss and hunting. Habitat loss has been caused by the expansion of palm and rubber farming, and logging. Both activities clear out forests. The Bornean yellow muntjac is hunted for meat and its skin, as well as for use in traditional medicines.

In China, the giant panda was classified as Endangered in 1990. The Chinese introduced measures to decrease poaching and enlarge the pandas' habitat. After two decades, the pandas' status was upgraded to Vulnerable.

Grizzly Bears Need You!

What can you do to help the bears? If you visit an area where grizzly bears live, there are some things you should know. Always travel in a group when hiking, and make noise. Some hikers wear bear bells so that bears know they are around, and many carry bear spray. Bears remember where they find food, so campers should store and clean up food properly so that bears are not attracted to their campsite. Also, respect signs about bear activity, such as warnings that an aggressive bear is nearby.

Rangers at Yellowstone National Park help enforce rules to protect grizzly bears. They also advise visitors on which parts of the park might not be accessible. This protects bears, because if bears attack people, the animals often have to be removed from the area or even killed.

If you live close to a bear habitat, learn about things that might attract bears onto your property. Do not leave pet food or garbage outside. Make sure that composting, bird feeders, beehives, and orchards are in secure areas.

SPREAD THE WORD

You might not live or travel in areas where grizzly bears live, so what can you do? Spreading information and educating people is a great way to help. Here are some ideas you can try:

- Take action! If you feel strongly about protecting grizzlies and other endangered species, write your elected representatives and make the case for protecting natural habitats.

- Contact a conservation organization such as Defenders of Wildlife and see how you can help it by raising funds through bake sales or other activities.

- Make up a poem or song about why it's important to be bear aware, using sound effects and actions. Get your whole class involved and perform it at assembly!

- Design a poster about responsible behavior around bears. Ask permission to put it up at school or in your local library or community center.

Learning More

Books

Markle, Sandra. *Grizzly Bears*. *Animal Predators*. Lerner Publishing Group, 2009.

O'Neal, Claire. *Yellowstone*. *Walk on the Wild Side: The National Parks*. Purple Toad Publishing, 2017.

Polydoros, Lori. *Grizzly Bears on the Hunt*. *Killer Animals*. Capstone Press, 2009.

Sartore, Joel. *Face to Face with Grizzlies*. *Face to Face with Animals*. National Geographic Children's Books, 2009.

Stanley, Joseph. *Grizzly Bear*. *North America's Biggest Beasts*. PowerKids Press, 2016.

On the Web

https://defenders.org/bear-awareness-week
With photographs, videos, and facts, this site provides information about bears and other animals, and the work of Defenders of Wildlife.

www.nps.gov/subjects/bears/teacherskids.htm
The National Park Service site has information about bears, plus links to videos and other resources.

www.bearsmart.com/about-bears/kids-and-teachers
A site for teachers and children with information about how to behave in areas with bears.

www.grizzlydiscoveryctr.org
A site with information about grizzly bears and other predators, as well as conservation efforts at Yellowstone National Park.

For videos, activities, and more, enter the access code at the Crabtree Plus website below.

www.crabtreeplus.com/animals-back-brink

Access code: abb37

Glossary

artificial Not natural

captivity Being kept in one place and being unable to leave

carcasses Remains of dead animals

carrion Dead and decaying animals

compensation Money paid in return for something that has been damaged or destroyed

conservation Preserving and using resources wisely

cultivation The artificial growing of plants, such as crops

decline A fall in the quantity of something

delisted Removed as an entry from a list

ecosystem All living things in a particular area and how they interact

extinct Describes a species that no longer survives

foraging Searching for food

genetic Passed on from one generation to the next

habitat The conditions in which an animal or plant naturally lives

industrial Relating to industry, or the manufacturing of goods to be sold

life cycle The complete set of changes through which a creature lives, such as birth, youth, adulthood, reproduction, and death

livestock Farm animals, such as sheep or cows

monitor To observe and record information about a subject

natural resources Useful materials that occur in nature

nuisance Something that causes a problem

omnivores Animals that eat meat, fish, and plants

penalties Punishments imposed for breaking a rule or law

poaching Illegal hunting

predators Animals that hunt other animals for food

prey Animals that are hunted by other animals

range The extent of the area in which an animal naturally lives

reclusive Preferring to be alone

scavenger Describes an animal that feeds on dead creatures or carcasses killed by other animals

self-sustaining Being able to live healthily without help from humans

sow An adult female bear

species A group of animals or plants that are similar to each other

tranquilized Given a drug that causes calmness

trapping Catching animals, often for their fur or meat

umbrella species Species whose health is a sign of the health of a whole ecosystem

ungulate A hoofed mammal such as an elk or deer

wilderness An area that is wild and uninhabited

Index and About the Author

ABOUT THE AUTHOR

Ruth Daly has more than 25 years teaching experience, mainly in elementary schools, and she currently teaches Grade 3. She has written more than 30 nonfiction books for the education market on a wide range of subjects and for a variety of age groups. These include books on animals, life cycles, and the natural environment. Her fiction and poetry have been published in magazines and literary journals.